MW01282022

This
Book Review
Log Book
Belongs To:

_____

_____

_____

NUMBER	BOOK TITLE	AUTHOR NAME	RATING
1			☆ ☆ ☆ ☆ ☆
2			☆ ☆ ☆ ☆ ☆
3			☆ ☆ ☆ ☆ ☆
4			☆ ☆ ☆ ☆ ☆
5			☆ ☆ ☆ ☆ ☆
6			☆ ☆ ☆ ☆ ☆
7			☆ ☆ ☆ ☆ ☆
8			☆ ☆ ☆ ☆ ☆
9			☆ ☆ ☆ ☆ ☆
10			☆ ☆ ☆ ☆ ☆
11			☆ ☆ ☆ ☆ ☆
12			☆ ☆ ☆ ☆ ☆
13			☆ ☆ ☆ ☆ ☆
14			☆ ☆ ☆ ☆ ☆
15			☆ ☆ ☆ ☆ ☆
16			☆ ☆ ☆ ☆ ☆
17			☆ ☆ ☆ ☆ ☆
18			☆ ☆ ☆ ☆ ☆
19			☆ ☆ ☆ ☆ ☆
20			☆ ☆ ☆ ☆ ☆
21			☆ ☆ ☆ ☆ ☆
22			☆ ☆ ☆ ☆ ☆
23			☆ ☆ ☆ ☆ ☆
24			☆ ☆ ☆ ☆ ☆
25			☆ ☆ ☆ ☆ ☆

NUMBER	BOOK TITLE	AUTHOR NAME	RATING
26			☆ ☆ ☆ ☆ ☆
27			☆ ☆ ☆ ☆ ☆
28			☆ ☆ ☆ ☆ ☆
29			☆ ☆ ☆ ☆ ☆
30			☆ ☆ ☆ ☆ ☆
31			☆ ☆ ☆ ☆ ☆
32			☆ ☆ ☆ ☆ ☆
33			☆ ☆ ☆ ☆ ☆
34			☆ ☆ ☆ ☆ ☆
35			☆ ☆ ☆ ☆ ☆
36			☆ ☆ ☆ ☆ ☆
37			☆ ☆ ☆ ☆ ☆
38			☆ ☆ ☆ ☆ ☆
39			☆ ☆ ☆ ☆ ☆
40			☆ ☆ ☆ ☆ ☆
41			☆ ☆ ☆ ☆ ☆
42			☆ ☆ ☆ ☆ ☆
43			☆ ☆ ☆ ☆ ☆
44			☆ ☆ ☆ ☆ ☆
45			☆ ☆ ☆ ☆ ☆
46			☆ ☆ ☆ ☆ ☆
47			☆ ☆ ☆ ☆ ☆
48			☆ ☆ ☆ ☆ ☆
49			☆ ☆ ☆ ☆ ☆
50			☆ ☆ ☆ ☆ ☆

NUMBER	BOOK TITLE	AUTHOR NAME	RATING
51			☆ ☆ ☆ ☆ ☆
52			☆ ☆ ☆ ☆ ☆
53			☆ ☆ ☆ ☆ ☆
54			☆ ☆ ☆ ☆ ☆
55			☆ ☆ ☆ ☆ ☆
56			☆ ☆ ☆ ☆ ☆
57			☆ ☆ ☆ ☆ ☆
58			☆ ☆ ☆ ☆ ☆
59			☆ ☆ ☆ ☆ ☆
60			☆ ☆ ☆ ☆ ☆
61			☆ ☆ ☆ ☆ ☆
62			☆ ☆ ☆ ☆ ☆
63			☆ ☆ ☆ ☆ ☆
64			☆ ☆ ☆ ☆ ☆
65			☆ ☆ ☆ ☆ ☆
66			☆ ☆ ☆ ☆ ☆
67			☆ ☆ ☆ ☆ ☆
68			☆ ☆ ☆ ☆ ☆
69			☆ ☆ ☆ ☆ ☆
70			☆ ☆ ☆ ☆ ☆
71			☆ ☆ ☆ ☆ ☆
72			☆ ☆ ☆ ☆ ☆
73			☆ ☆ ☆ ☆ ☆
74			☆ ☆ ☆ ☆ ☆
75			☆ ☆ ☆ ☆ ☆

NUMBER	BOOK TITLE	AUTHOR NAME	RATING
76			☆ ☆ ☆ ☆ ☆
77			☆ ☆ ☆ ☆ ☆
78			☆ ☆ ☆ ☆ ☆
79			☆ ☆ ☆ ☆ ☆
80			☆ ☆ ☆ ☆ ☆
81			☆ ☆ ☆ ☆ ☆
82			☆ ☆ ☆ ☆ ☆
83			☆ ☆ ☆ ☆ ☆
84			☆ ☆ ☆ ☆ ☆
85			☆ ☆ ☆ ☆ ☆
86			☆ ☆ ☆ ☆ ☆
87			☆ ☆ ☆ ☆ ☆
88			☆ ☆ ☆ ☆ ☆
89			☆ ☆ ☆ ☆ ☆
90			☆ ☆ ☆ ☆ ☆
91			☆ ☆ ☆ ☆ ☆
92			☆ ☆ ☆ ☆ ☆
93			☆ ☆ ☆ ☆ ☆
94			☆ ☆ ☆ ☆ ☆
95			☆ ☆ ☆ ☆ ☆
96			☆ ☆ ☆ ☆ ☆
97			☆ ☆ ☆ ☆ ☆
98			☆ ☆ ☆ ☆ ☆
99			☆ ☆ ☆ ☆ ☆
100			☆ ☆ ☆ ☆ ☆

TITLE:_____ PUB DATE:_____

AUTHOR:_____ PAGE COUNT:_____

DATE STARTED:_____ DATE FINISHED:_____

GENRE		☆ ☆ ☆ ☆ ☆
CHARACTERS		☆ ☆ ☆ ☆ ☆
PLOT STORY		☆ ☆ ☆ ☆ ☆
READABILITY SCORE		☆ ☆ ☆ ☆ ☆
SUBJECT		☆ ☆ ☆ ☆ ☆

NOTES

FAVORITE QUOTES OF THIS BOOK:

HARDCOVER ☐   PAPERBACK ☐   EBOOK ☐   AUDIOBOOK ☐

OVERALL RATING: ☆ ☆ ☆ ☆ ☆   1

TITLE:_____ PUB DATE:_____

AUTHOR:_____ PAGE COUNT:_____

DATE STARTED:_____ DATE FINISHED:_____

GENRE		☆ ☆ ☆ ☆ ☆
CHARACTERS		☆ ☆ ☆ ☆ ☆
PLOT STORY		☆ ☆ ☆ ☆ ☆
READABILITY SCORE		☆ ☆ ☆ ☆ ☆
SUBJECT		☆ ☆ ☆ ☆ ☆

NOTES

FAVORITE QUOTES OF THIS BOOK:

HARDCOVER ☐   PAPERBACK ☐   EBOOK ☐   AUDIOBOOK ☐

OVERALL RATING: ☆ ☆ ☆ ☆ ☆

TITLE: _____ PUB DATE: _____

AUTHOR: _____ PAGE COUNT: _____

DATE STARTED: _____ DATE FINISHED: _____

GENRE		☆ ☆ ☆ ☆ ☆
CHARACTERS		☆ ☆ ☆ ☆ ☆
PLOT STORY		☆ ☆ ☆ ☆ ☆
READABILITY SCORE		☆ ☆ ☆ ☆ ☆
SUBJECT		☆ ☆ ☆ ☆ ☆

NOTES

FAVORITE QUOTES OF THIS BOOK:

HARDCOVER ☐   PAPERBACK ☐   EBOOK ☐   AUDIOBOOK ☐

OVERALL RATING: ☆ ☆ ☆ ☆ ☆   3

TITLE:_____ PUB DATE:_____

AUTHOR:_____ PAGE COUNT:_____

DATE STARTED:_____ DATE FINISHED:_____

GENRE		☆ ☆ ☆ ☆ ☆
CHARACTERS		☆ ☆ ☆ ☆ ☆
PLOT STORY		☆ ☆ ☆ ☆ ☆
READABILITY SCORE		☆ ☆ ☆ ☆ ☆
SUBJECT		☆ ☆ ☆ ☆ ☆

NOTES

FAVORITE QUOTES OF THIS BOOK:

HARDCOVER ☐   PAPERBACK ☐   EBOOK ☐   AUDIOBOOK ☐

OVERALL RATING: ☆ ☆ ☆ ☆ ☆   4

TITLE:	PUB DATE:	
AUTHOR:	PAGE COUNT:	
DATE STARTED:	DATE FINISHED:	

GENRE		☆ ☆ ☆ ☆ ☆
CHARACTERS		☆ ☆ ☆ ☆ ☆
PLOT STORY		☆ ☆ ☆ ☆ ☆
READABILITY SCORE		☆ ☆ ☆ ☆ ☆
SUBJECT		☆ ☆ ☆ ☆ ☆

NOTES

FAVORITE QUOTES OF THIS BOOK:

HARDCOVER ☐   PAPERBACK ☐   EBOOK ☐   AUDIOBOOK ☐

OVERALL RATING: ☆ ☆ ☆ ☆ ☆   5

TITLE:_____ PUB DATE:_____

AUTHOR:_____ PAGE COUNT:_____

DATE STARTED:_____ DATE FINISHED:_____

GENRE		☆ ☆ ☆ ☆ ☆
CHARACTERS		☆ ☆ ☆ ☆ ☆
PLOT STORY		☆ ☆ ☆ ☆ ☆
READABILITY SCORE		☆ ☆ ☆ ☆ ☆
SUBJECT		☆ ☆ ☆ ☆ ☆

NOTES

FAVORITE QUOTES OF THIS BOOK:

HARDCOVER ☐   PAPERBACK ☐   EBOOK ☐   AUDIOBOOK ☐

OVERALL RATING: ☆ ☆ ☆ ☆ ☆

TITLE:_____ PUB DATE:_____

AUTHOR:_____ PAGE COUNT:_____

DATE STARTED:_____ DATE FINISHED:_____

GENRE		☆ ☆ ☆ ☆ ☆
CHARACTERS		☆ ☆ ☆ ☆ ☆
PLOT STORY		☆ ☆ ☆ ☆ ☆
READABILITY SCORE		☆ ☆ ☆ ☆ ☆
SUBJECT		☆ ☆ ☆ ☆ ☆

NOTES

FAVORITE QUOTES OF THIS BOOK:

HARDCOVER ☐   PAPERBACK ☐   EBOOK ☐   AUDIOBOOK ☐

OVERALL RATING: ☆ ☆ ☆ ☆ ☆

TITLE:_____ PUB DATE:_____

AUTHOR:_____ PAGE COUNT:_____

DATE STARTED:_____ DATE FINISHED:_____

GENRE		☆ ☆ ☆ ☆ ☆
CHARACTERS		☆ ☆ ☆ ☆ ☆
PLOT STORY		☆ ☆ ☆ ☆ ☆
READABILITY SCORE		☆ ☆ ☆ ☆ ☆
SUBJECT		☆ ☆ ☆ ☆ ☆

NOTES

FAVORITE QUOTES OF THIS BOOK:

HARDCOVER ☐   PAPERBACK ☐   EBOOK ☐   AUDIOBOOK ☐

OVERALL RATING: ☆ ☆ ☆ ☆ ☆   8

TITLE:_____   PUB DATE:_____

AUTHOR:_____   PAGE COUNT:_____

DATE STARTED:_____   DATE FINISHED:_____

GENRE		☆ ☆ ☆ ☆ ☆
CHARACTERS		☆ ☆ ☆ ☆ ☆
PLOT STORY		☆ ☆ ☆ ☆ ☆
READABILITY SCORE		☆ ☆ ☆ ☆ ☆
SUBJECT		☆ ☆ ☆ ☆ ☆

NOTES

FAVORITE QUOTES OF THIS BOOK:

HARDCOVER ☐   PAPERBACK ☐   EBOOK ☐   AUDIOBOOK ☐

OVERALL RATING: ☆ ☆ ☆ ☆ ☆

TITLE: _____ PUB DATE: _____

AUTHOR: _____ PAGE COUNT: _____

DATE STARTED: _____ DATE FINISHED: _____

GENRE		☆ ☆ ☆ ☆ ☆
CHARACTERS		☆ ☆ ☆ ☆ ☆
PLOT STORY		☆ ☆ ☆ ☆ ☆
READABILITY SCORE		☆ ☆ ☆ ☆ ☆
SUBJECT		☆ ☆ ☆ ☆ ☆

NOTES

FAVORITE QUOTES OF THIS BOOK:

HARDCOVER ☐　　　PAPERBACK ☐　　　EBOOK ☐　　　AUDIOBOOK ☐

OVERALL RATING: ☆ ☆ ☆ ☆ ☆

TITLE:_____ PUB DATE:_____

AUTHOR:_____ PAGE COUNT:_____

DATE STARTED:_____ DATE FINISHED:_____

GENRE		☆ ☆ ☆ ☆ ☆
CHARACTERS		☆ ☆ ☆ ☆ ☆
PLOT STORY		☆ ☆ ☆ ☆ ☆
READABILITY SCORE		☆ ☆ ☆ ☆ ☆
SUBJECT		☆ ☆ ☆ ☆ ☆

NOTES

FAVORITE QUOTES OF THIS BOOK:

HARDCOVER ☐   PAPERBACK ☐   EBOOK ☐   AUDIOBOOK ☐

OVERALL RATING: ☆ ☆ ☆ ☆ ☆   11

TITLE: _____ PUB DATE: _____

AUTHOR: _____ PAGE COUNT: _____

DATE STARTED: _____ DATE FINISHED: _____

GENRE		☆ ☆ ☆ ☆ ☆
CHARACTERS		☆ ☆ ☆ ☆ ☆
PLOT STORY		☆ ☆ ☆ ☆ ☆
READABILITY SCORE		☆ ☆ ☆ ☆ ☆
SUBJECT		☆ ☆ ☆ ☆ ☆

NOTES

FAVORITE QUOTES OF THIS BOOK:

HARDCOVER ☐   PAPERBACK ☐   EBOOK ☐   AUDIOBOOK ☐

OVERALL RATING: ☆ ☆ ☆ ☆ ☆   12

TITLE: _____ PUB DATE: _____

AUTHOR: _____ PAGE COUNT: _____

DATE STARTED: _____ DATE FINISHED: _____

GENRE		☆ ☆ ☆ ☆ ☆
CHARACTERS		☆ ☆ ☆ ☆ ☆
PLOT STORY		☆ ☆ ☆ ☆ ☆
READABILITY SCORE		☆ ☆ ☆ ☆ ☆
SUBJECT		☆ ☆ ☆ ☆ ☆

NOTES

FAVORITE QUOTES OF THIS BOOK:

HARDCOVER ☐   PAPERBACK ☐   EBOOK ☐   AUDIOBOOK ☐

OVERALL RATING: ☆ ☆ ☆ ☆ ☆

TITLE:_____ PUB DATE:_____

AUTHOR:_____ PAGE COUNT:_____

DATE STARTED:_____ DATE FINISHED:_____

GENRE		☆ ☆ ☆ ☆ ☆
CHARACTERS		☆ ☆ ☆ ☆ ☆
PLOT STORY		☆ ☆ ☆ ☆ ☆
READABILITY SCORE		☆ ☆ ☆ ☆ ☆
SUBJECT		☆ ☆ ☆ ☆ ☆

NOTES

FAVORITE QUOTES OF THIS BOOK:

HARDCOVER ☐   PAPERBACK ☐   EBOOK ☐   AUDIOBOOK ☐

OVERALL RATING: ☆ ☆ ☆ ☆ ☆   14

TITLE: _____ PUB DATE: _____

AUTHOR: _____ PAGE COUNT: _____

DATE STARTED: _____ DATE FINISHED: _____

GENRE		☆ ☆ ☆ ☆ ☆
CHARACTERS		☆ ☆ ☆ ☆ ☆
PLOT STORY		☆ ☆ ☆ ☆ ☆
READABILITY SCORE		☆ ☆ ☆ ☆ ☆
SUBJECT		☆ ☆ ☆ ☆ ☆

NOTES

FAVORITE QUOTES OF THIS BOOK:

HARDCOVER ☐   PAPERBACK ☐   EBOOK ☐   AUDIOBOOK ☐

OVERALL RATING: ☆ ☆ ☆ ☆ ☆

TITLE:_____ PUB DATE:_____

AUTHOR:_____ PAGE COUNT:_____

DATE STARTED:_____ DATE FINISHED:_____

GENRE		☆ ☆ ☆ ☆ ☆
CHARACTERS		☆ ☆ ☆ ☆ ☆
PLOT STORY		☆ ☆ ☆ ☆ ☆
READABILITY SCORE		☆ ☆ ☆ ☆ ☆
SUBJECT		☆ ☆ ☆ ☆ ☆

NOTES

FAVORITE QUOTES OF THIS BOOK:

HARDCOVER ☐   PAPERBACK ☐   EBOOK ☐   AUDIOBOOK ☐

OVERALL RATING: ☆ ☆ ☆ ☆ ☆   16

TITLE: _____ PUB DATE: _____

AUTHOR: _____ PAGE COUNT: _____

DATE STARTED: _____ DATE FINISHED: _____

GENERE		☆ ☆ ☆ ☆ ☆
CHARACTERS		☆ ☆ ☆ ☆ ☆
PLOT STORY		☆ ☆ ☆ ☆ ☆
READABILITY SCORE		☆ ☆ ☆ ☆ ☆
SUBJECT		☆ ☆ ☆ ☆ ☆

NOTES

FAVORITE QUOTES OF THIS BOOK:

HARDCOVER ☐   PAPERBACK ☐   EBOOK ☐   AUDIOBOOK ☐

OVERALL RATING: ☆ ☆ ☆ ☆ ☆

TITLE: _____ PUB DATE: _____

AUTHOR: _____ PAGE COUNT: _____

DATE STARTED: _____ DATE FINISHED: _____

GENRE		☆ ☆ ☆ ☆ ☆
CHARACTERS		☆ ☆ ☆ ☆ ☆
PLOT STORY		☆ ☆ ☆ ☆ ☆
READABILITY SCORE		☆ ☆ ☆ ☆ ☆
SUBJECT		☆ ☆ ☆ ☆ ☆

NOTES

FAVORITE QUOTES OF THIS BOOK:

HARDCOVER ☐   PAPERBACK ☐   EBOOK ☐   AUDIOBOOK ☐

OVERALL RATING: ☆ ☆ ☆ ☆ ☆   18

TITLE: _____ PUB DATE: _____

AUTHOR: _____ PAGE COUNT: _____

DATE STARTED: _____ DATE FINISHED: _____

GENRE		☆ ☆ ☆ ☆ ☆
CHARACTERS		☆ ☆ ☆ ☆ ☆
PLOT STORY		☆ ☆ ☆ ☆ ☆
READABILITY SCORE		☆ ☆ ☆ ☆ ☆
SUBJECT		☆ ☆ ☆ ☆ ☆

NOTES

FAVORITE QUOTES OF THIS BOOK:

HARDCOVER ☐   PAPERBACK ☐   EBOOK ☐   AUDIOBOOK ☐

OVERALL RATING: ☆ ☆ ☆ ☆ ☆

TITLE:_____ PUB DATE:_____

AUTHOR:_____ PAGE COUNT:_____

DATE STARTED:_____ DATE FINISHED:_____

GENRE		☆ ☆ ☆ ☆ ☆
CHARACTERS		☆ ☆ ☆ ☆ ☆
PLOT STORY		☆ ☆ ☆ ☆ ☆
READABILITY SCORE		☆ ☆ ☆ ☆ ☆
SUBJECT		☆ ☆ ☆ ☆ ☆

NOTES

FAVORITE QUOTES OF THIS BOOK:

HARDCOVER ☐   PAPERBACK ☐   EBOOK ☐   AUDIOBOOK ☐

OVERALL RATING: ☆ ☆ ☆ ☆ ☆   20

TITLE:_____ PUB DATE:_____

AUTHOR:_____ PAGE COUNT:_____

DATE STARTED:_____ DATE FINISHED:_____

GENRE		☆ ☆ ☆ ☆ ☆
CHARACTERS		☆ ☆ ☆ ☆ ☆
PLOT STORY		☆ ☆ ☆ ☆ ☆
READABILITY SCORE		☆ ☆ ☆ ☆ ☆
SUBJECT		☆ ☆ ☆ ☆ ☆

NOTES

FAVORITE QUOTES OF THIS BOOK:

HARDCOVER ☐   PAPERBACK ☐   EBOOK ☐   AUDIOBOOK ☐

OVERALL RATING: ☆ ☆ ☆ ☆ ☆

TITLE:_____ PUB DATE:_____

AUTHOR:_____ PAGE COUNT:_____

DATE STARTED:_____ DATE FINISHED:_____

GENRE		☆ ☆ ☆ ☆ ☆
CHARACTERS		☆ ☆ ☆ ☆ ☆
PLOT STORY		☆ ☆ ☆ ☆ ☆
READABILITY SCORE		☆ ☆ ☆ ☆ ☆
SUBJECT		☆ ☆ ☆ ☆ ☆

NOTES

FAVORITE QUOTES OF THIS BOOK:

HARDCOVER ☐   PAPERBACK ☐   EBOOK ☐   AUDIOBOOK ☐

OVERALL RATING: ☆ ☆ ☆ ☆ ☆

TITLE:	PUB DATE:	
AUTHOR:	PAGE COUNT:	
DATE STARTED:	DATE FINISHED:	

GENRE		☆ ☆ ☆ ☆ ☆
CHARACTERS		☆ ☆ ☆ ☆ ☆
PLOT STORY		☆ ☆ ☆ ☆ ☆
READABILITY SCORE		☆ ☆ ☆ ☆ ☆
SUBJECT		☆ ☆ ☆ ☆ ☆

NOTES

FAVORITE QUOTES OF THIS BOOK:

HARDCOVER ☐   PAPERBACK ☐   EBOOK ☐   AUDIOBOOK ☐

OVERALL RATING: ☆ ☆ ☆ ☆ ☆   23

TITLE: _____ PUB DATE: _____

AUTHOR: _____ PAGE COUNT: _____

DATE STARTED: _____ DATE FINISHED: _____

GENRE		☆ ☆ ☆ ☆ ☆
CHARACTERS		☆ ☆ ☆ ☆ ☆
PLOT STORY		☆ ☆ ☆ ☆ ☆
READABILITY SCORE		☆ ☆ ☆ ☆ ☆
SUBJECT		☆ ☆ ☆ ☆ ☆

NOTES

FAVORITE QUOTES OF THIS BOOK:

HARDCOVER ☐   PAPERBACK ☐   EBOOK ☐   AUDIOBOOK ☐

OVERALL RATING: ☆ ☆ ☆ ☆ ☆   24

TITLE: _____ PUB DATE: _____

AUTHOR: _____ PAGE COUNT: _____

DATE STARTED: _____ DATE FINISHED: _____

GENRE		☆ ☆ ☆ ☆ ☆
CHARACTERS		☆ ☆ ☆ ☆ ☆
PLOT STORY		☆ ☆ ☆ ☆ ☆
READABILITY SCORE		☆ ☆ ☆ ☆ ☆
SUBJECT		☆ ☆ ☆ ☆ ☆

NOTES

FAVORITE QUOTES OF THIS BOOK:

HARDCOVER ☐   PAPERBACK ☐   EBOOK ☐   AUDIOBOOK ☐

OVERALL RATING: ☆ ☆ ☆ ☆ ☆

TITLE: _____ PUB DATE: _____

AUTHOR: _____ PAGE COUNT: _____

DATE STARTED: _____ DATE FINISHED: _____

GENRE		☆ ☆ ☆ ☆ ☆
CHARACTERS		☆ ☆ ☆ ☆ ☆
PLOT STORY		☆ ☆ ☆ ☆ ☆
READABILITY SCORE		☆ ☆ ☆ ☆ ☆
SUBJECT		☆ ☆ ☆ ☆ ☆

NOTES

FAVORITE QUOTES OF THIS BOOK:

HARDCOVER ☐   PAPERBACK ☐   EBOOK ☐   AUDIOBOOK ☐

OVERALL RATING: ☆ ☆ ☆ ☆ ☆

TITLE:_____ PUB DATE:_____

AUTHOR:_____ PAGE COUNT:_____

DATE STARTED:_____ DATE FINISHED:_____

GENRE		☆ ☆ ☆ ☆ ☆
CHARACTERS		☆ ☆ ☆ ☆ ☆
PLOT STORY		☆ ☆ ☆ ☆ ☆
READABILITY SCORE		☆ ☆ ☆ ☆ ☆
SUBJECT		☆ ☆ ☆ ☆ ☆

NOTES

FAVORITE QUOTES OF THIS BOOK:

HARDCOVER ☐   PAPERBACK ☐   EBOOK ☐   AUDIOBOOK ☐

OVERALL RATING: ☆ ☆ ☆ ☆ ☆

TITLE:_____ PUB DATE:_____

AUTHOR:_____ PAGE COUNT:_____

DATE STARTED:_____ DATE FINISHED:_____

GENRE		☆ ☆ ☆ ☆ ☆
CHARACTERS		☆ ☆ ☆ ☆ ☆
PLOT STORY		☆ ☆ ☆ ☆ ☆
READABILITY SCORE		☆ ☆ ☆ ☆ ☆
SUBJECT		☆ ☆ ☆ ☆ ☆

NOTES

FAVORITE QUOTES OF THIS BOOK:

HARDCOVER ☐   PAPERBACK ☐   EBOOK ☐   AUDIOBOOK ☐

OVERALL RATING: ☆ ☆ ☆ ☆ ☆

TITLE:_____ PUB DATE:_____

AUTHOR:_____ PAGE COUNT:_____

DATE STARTED:_____ DATE FINISHED:_____

GENRE		☆ ☆ ☆ ☆ ☆
CHARACTERS		☆ ☆ ☆ ☆ ☆
PLOT STORY		☆ ☆ ☆ ☆ ☆
READABILITY SCORE		☆ ☆ ☆ ☆ ☆
SUBJECT		☆ ☆ ☆ ☆ ☆

NOTES

FAVORITE QUOTES OF THIS BOOK:

HARDCOVER ☐   PAPERBACK ☐   EBOOK ☐   AUDIOBOOK ☐

OVERALL RATING: ☆ ☆ ☆ ☆ ☆

TITLE:_____ PUB DATE:_____

AUTHOR:_____ PAGE COUNT:_____

DATE STARTED:_____ DATE FINISHED:_____

GENRE		☆ ☆ ☆ ☆ ☆
CHARACTERS		☆ ☆ ☆ ☆ ☆
PLOT STORY		☆ ☆ ☆ ☆ ☆
READABILITY SCORE		☆ ☆ ☆ ☆ ☆
SUBJECT		☆ ☆ ☆ ☆ ☆

NOTES

FAVORITE QUOTES OF THIS BOOK:

HARDCOVER ☐   PAPERBACK ☐   EBOOK ☐   AUDIOBOOK ☐

OVERALL RATING: ☆ ☆ ☆ ☆ ☆   30

TITLE: _____ PUB DATE: _____

AUTHOR: _____ PAGE COUNT: _____

DATE STARTED: _____ DATE FINISHED: _____

GENRE		☆ ☆ ☆ ☆ ☆
CHARACTERS		☆ ☆ ☆ ☆ ☆
PLOT STORY		☆ ☆ ☆ ☆ ☆
READABILITY SCORE		☆ ☆ ☆ ☆ ☆
SUBJECT		☆ ☆ ☆ ☆ ☆

NOTES

FAVORITE QUOTES OF THIS BOOK:

HARDCOVER ☐   PAPERBACK ☐   EBOOK ☐   AUDIOBOOK ☐

OVERALL RATING: ☆ ☆ ☆ ☆ ☆   31

TITLE:_____ PUB DATE:_____

AUTHOR:_____ PAGE COUNT:_____

DATE STARTED:_____ DATE FINISHED:_____

GENRE		☆ ☆ ☆ ☆ ☆
CHARACTERS		☆ ☆ ☆ ☆ ☆
PLOT STORY		☆ ☆ ☆ ☆ ☆
READABILITY SCORE		☆ ☆ ☆ ☆ ☆
SUBJECT		☆ ☆ ☆ ☆ ☆

NOTES

FAVORITE QUOTES OF THIS BOOK:

HARDCOVER ☐   PAPERBACK ☐   EBOOK ☐   AUDIOBOOK ☐

OVERALL RATING: ☆ ☆ ☆ ☆ ☆

TITLE:_____ PUB DATE:_____

AUTHOR:_____ PAGE COUNT:_____

DATE STARTED:_____ DATE FINISHED:_____

GENRE		☆ ☆ ☆ ☆ ☆
CHARACTERS		☆ ☆ ☆ ☆ ☆
PLOT STORY		☆ ☆ ☆ ☆ ☆
READABILITY SCORE		☆ ☆ ☆ ☆ ☆
SUBJECT		☆ ☆ ☆ ☆ ☆

NOTES

FAVORITE QUOTES OF THIS BOOK:

HARDCOVER ☐   PAPERBACK ☐   EBOOK ☐   AUDIOBOOK ☐

OVERALL RATING: ☆ ☆ ☆ ☆ ☆

TITLE:_____ PUB DATE:_____

AUTHOR:_____ PAGE COUNT:_____

DATE STARTED:_____ DATE FINISHED:_____

GENRE		☆ ☆ ☆ ☆ ☆
CHARACTERS		☆ ☆ ☆ ☆ ☆
PLOT STORY		☆ ☆ ☆ ☆ ☆
READABILITY SCORE		☆ ☆ ☆ ☆ ☆
SUBJECT		☆ ☆ ☆ ☆ ☆

NOTES

FAVORITE QUOTES OF THIS BOOK:

HARDCOVER ☐   PAPERBACK ☐   EBOOK ☐   AUDIOBOOK ☐

OVERALL RATING: ☆ ☆ ☆ ☆ ☆   34

TITLE:	PUB DATE:	
AUTHOR:	PAGE COUNT:	
DATE STARTED:	DATE FINISHED:	

GENRE		☆ ☆ ☆ ☆ ☆
CHARACTERS		☆ ☆ ☆ ☆ ☆
PLOT STORY		☆ ☆ ☆ ☆ ☆
READABILITY SCORE		☆ ☆ ☆ ☆ ☆
SUBJECT		☆ ☆ ☆ ☆ ☆

NOTES

FAVORITE QUOTES OF THIS BOOK:

HARDCOVER ☐   PAPERBACK ☐   EBOOK ☐   AUDIOBOOK ☐

OVERALL RATING: ☆ ☆ ☆ ☆ ☆

TITLE:_____ PUB DATE:_____

AUTHOR:_____ PAGE COUNT:_____

DATE STARTED:_____ DATE FINISHED:_____

GENRE		☆ ☆ ☆ ☆ ☆
CHARACTERS		☆ ☆ ☆ ☆ ☆
PLOT STORY		☆ ☆ ☆ ☆ ☆
READABILITY SCORE		☆ ☆ ☆ ☆ ☆
SUBJECT		☆ ☆ ☆ ☆ ☆

NOTES

FAVORITE QUOTES OF THIS BOOK:

HARDCOVER ☐   PAPERBACK ☐   EBOOK ☐   AUDIOBOOK ☐

OVERALL RATING: ☆ ☆ ☆ ☆ ☆   36

TITLE:_____ PUB DATE:_____

AUTHOR:_____ PAGE COUNT:_____

DATE STARTED:_____ DATE FINISHED:_____

GENRE		☆ ☆ ☆ ☆ ☆
CHARACTERS		☆ ☆ ☆ ☆ ☆
PLOT STORY		☆ ☆ ☆ ☆ ☆
READABILITY SCORE		☆ ☆ ☆ ☆ ☆
SUBJECT		☆ ☆ ☆ ☆ ☆

NOTES

FAVORITE QUOTES OF THIS BOOK:

HARDCOVER ☐   PAPERBACK ☐   EBOOK ☐   AUDIOBOOK ☐

OVERALL RATING: ☆ ☆ ☆ ☆ ☆

TITLE:_____ PUB DATE:_____

AUTHOR:_____ PAGE COUNT:_____

DATE STARTED:_____ DATE FINISHED:_____

GENRE		☆ ☆ ☆ ☆ ☆
CHARACTERS		☆ ☆ ☆ ☆ ☆
PLOT STORY		☆ ☆ ☆ ☆ ☆
READABILITY SCORE		☆ ☆ ☆ ☆ ☆
SUBJECT		☆ ☆ ☆ ☆ ☆

NOTES

FAVORITE QUOTES OF THIS BOOK:

HARDCOVER ☐   PAPERBACK ☐   EBOOK ☐   AUDIOBOOK ☐

OVERALL RATING: ☆ ☆ ☆ ☆ ☆   38

TITLE:_____ PUB DATE:_____

AUTHOR:_____ PAGE COUNT:_____

DATE STARTED:_____ DATE FINISHED:_____

GENRE		☆ ☆ ☆ ☆ ☆
CHARACTERS		☆ ☆ ☆ ☆ ☆
PLOT STORY		☆ ☆ ☆ ☆ ☆
READABILITY SCORE		☆ ☆ ☆ ☆ ☆
SUBJECT		☆ ☆ ☆ ☆ ☆

NOTES

FAVORITE QUOTES OF THIS BOOK:

HARDCOVER ☐   PAPERBACK ☐   EBOOK ☐   AUDIOBOOK ☐

OVERALL RATING: ☆ ☆ ☆ ☆ ☆

TITLE:_____ PUB DATE:_____

AUTHOR:_____ PAGE COUNT:_____

DATE STARTED:_____ DATE FINISHED:_____

GENRE		☆ ☆ ☆ ☆ ☆
CHARACTERS		☆ ☆ ☆ ☆ ☆
PLOT STORY		☆ ☆ ☆ ☆ ☆
READABILITY SCORE		☆ ☆ ☆ ☆ ☆
SUBJECT		☆ ☆ ☆ ☆ ☆

NOTES

FAVORITE QUOTES OF THIS BOOK:

HARDCOVER ☐   PAPERBACK ☐   EBOOK ☐   AUDIOBOOK ☐

OVERALL RATING: ☆ ☆ ☆ ☆ ☆

TITLE:_____ PUB DATE:_____

AUTHOR:_____ PAGE COUNT:_____

DATE STARTED:_____ DATE FINISHED:_____

GENRE		☆ ☆ ☆ ☆ ☆
CHARACTERS		☆ ☆ ☆ ☆ ☆
PLOT STORY		☆ ☆ ☆ ☆ ☆
READABILITY SCORE		☆ ☆ ☆ ☆ ☆
SUBJECT		☆ ☆ ☆ ☆ ☆

NOTES

FAVORITE QUOTES OF THIS BOOK:

HARDCOVER ☐   PAPERBACK ☐   EBOOK ☐   AUDIOBOOK ☐

OVERALL RATING: ☆ ☆ ☆ ☆ ☆   41

TITLE:_____ PUB DATE:_____

AUTHOR:_____ PAGE COUNT:_____

DATE STARTED:_____ DATE FINISHED:_____

GENERE		☆ ☆ ☆ ☆ ☆
CHARACTERS		☆ ☆ ☆ ☆ ☆
PLOT STORY		☆ ☆ ☆ ☆ ☆
READABILITY SCORE		☆ ☆ ☆ ☆ ☆
SUBJECT		☆ ☆ ☆ ☆ ☆

NOTES

FAVORITE QUOTES OF THIS BOOK:

HARDCOVER ☐   PAPERBACK ☐   EBOOK ☐   AUDIOBOOK ☐

OVERALL RATING: ☆ ☆ ☆ ☆ ☆   42

TITLE:_____ PUB DATE:_____

AUTHOR:_____ PAGE COUNT:_____

DATE STARTED:_____ DATE FINISHED:_____

GENRE		☆ ☆ ☆ ☆ ☆
CHARACTERS		☆ ☆ ☆ ☆ ☆
PLOT STORY		☆ ☆ ☆ ☆ ☆
READABILITY SCORE		☆ ☆ ☆ ☆ ☆
SUBJECT		☆ ☆ ☆ ☆ ☆

NOTES

FAVORITE QUOTES OF THIS BOOK:

HARDCOVER ☐   PAPERBACK ☐   EBOOK ☐   AUDIOBOOK ☐

OVERALL RATING: ☆ ☆ ☆ ☆ ☆

TITLE: _____ PUB DATE: _____

AUTHOR: _____ PAGE COUNT: _____

DATE STARTED: _____ DATE FINISHED: _____

GENRE		☆ ☆ ☆ ☆ ☆
CHARACTERS		☆ ☆ ☆ ☆ ☆
PLOT STORY		☆ ☆ ☆ ☆ ☆
READABILITY SCORE		☆ ☆ ☆ ☆ ☆
SUBJECT		☆ ☆ ☆ ☆ ☆

NOTES

FAVORITE QUOTES OF THIS BOOK:

HARDCOVER ☐   PAPERBACK ☐   EBOOK ☐   AUDIOBOOK ☐

OVERALL RATING: ☆ ☆ ☆ ☆ ☆

TITLE:		PUB DATE:
AUTHOR:		PAGE COUNT:
DATE STARTED:	DATE FINISHED:	

GENRE		☆ ☆ ☆ ☆ ☆
CHARACTERS		☆ ☆ ☆ ☆ ☆
PLOT STORY		☆ ☆ ☆ ☆ ☆
READABILITY SCORE		☆ ☆ ☆ ☆ ☆
SUBJECT		☆ ☆ ☆ ☆ ☆

NOTES

FAVORITE QUOTES OF THIS BOOK:

HARDCOVER ☐   PAPERBACK ☐   EBOOK ☐   AUDIOBOOK ☐

OVERALL RATING: ☆ ☆ ☆ ☆ ☆   **45**

TITLE:_____ PUB DATE:_____

AUTHOR:_____ PAGE COUNT:_____

DATE STARTED:_____ DATE FINISHED:_____

GENRE		☆ ☆ ☆ ☆ ☆
CHARACTERS		☆ ☆ ☆ ☆ ☆
PLOT STORY		☆ ☆ ☆ ☆ ☆
READABILITY SCORE		☆ ☆ ☆ ☆ ☆
SUBJECT		☆ ☆ ☆ ☆ ☆

NOTES

FAVORITE QUOTES OF THIS BOOK:

HARDCOVER ☐   PAPERBACK ☐   EBOOK ☐   AUDIOBOOK ☐

OVERALL RATING: ☆ ☆ ☆ ☆ ☆

TITLE:		PUB DATE:
AUTHOR:		PAGE COUNT:
DATE STARTED:	DATE FINISHED:	

GENRE		☆ ☆ ☆ ☆ ☆
CHARACTERS		☆ ☆ ☆ ☆ ☆
PLOT STORY		☆ ☆ ☆ ☆ ☆
READABILITY SCORE		☆ ☆ ☆ ☆ ☆
SUBJECT		☆ ☆ ☆ ☆ ☆

NOTES

FAVORITE QUOTES OF THIS BOOK:

HARDCOVER ☐   PAPERBACK ☐   EBOOK ☐   AUDIOBOOK ☐

OVERALL RATING: ☆ ☆ ☆ ☆ ☆   47

TITLE:_____ PUB DATE:_____

AUTHOR:_____ PAGE COUNT:_____

DATE STARTED:_____ DATE FINISHED:_____

GENERE		☆ ☆ ☆ ☆ ☆
CHARACTERS		☆ ☆ ☆ ☆ ☆
PLOT STORY		☆ ☆ ☆ ☆ ☆
READABILITY SCORE		☆ ☆ ☆ ☆ ☆
SUBJECT		☆ ☆ ☆ ☆ ☆

NOTES

FAVORITE QUOTES OF THIS BOOK:

HARDCOVER ☐   PAPERBACK ☐   EBOOK ☐   AUDIOBOOK ☐

OVERALL RATING: ☆ ☆ ☆ ☆ ☆   48

TITLE: _____ PUB DATE: _____

AUTHOR: _____ PAGE COUNT: _____

DATE STARTED: _____ DATE FINISHED: _____

GENRE		☆ ☆ ☆ ☆ ☆
CHARACTERS		☆ ☆ ☆ ☆ ☆
PLOT STORY		☆ ☆ ☆ ☆ ☆
READABILITY SCORE		☆ ☆ ☆ ☆ ☆
SUBJECT		☆ ☆ ☆ ☆ ☆

NOTES

FAVORITE QUOTES OF THIS BOOK:

HARDCOVER ☐   PAPERBACK ☐   EBOOK ☐   AUDIOBOOK ☐

OVERALL RATING: ☆ ☆ ☆ ☆ ☆   49

TITLE:_____ PUB DATE:_____

AUTHOR:_____ PAGE COUNT:_____

DATE STARTED:_____ DATE FINISHED:_____

GENRE		☆ ☆ ☆ ☆ ☆
CHARACTERS		☆ ☆ ☆ ☆ ☆
PLOT STORY		☆ ☆ ☆ ☆ ☆
READABILITY SCORE		☆ ☆ ☆ ☆ ☆
SUBJECT		☆ ☆ ☆ ☆ ☆

NOTES

FAVORITE QUOTES OF THIS BOOK:

HARDCOVER ☐   PAPERBACK ☐   EBOOK ☐   AUDIOBOOK ☐

OVERALL RATING: ☆ ☆ ☆ ☆ ☆   50

TITLE:_____ PUB DATE:_____

AUTHOR:_____ PAGE COUNT:_____

DATE STARTED:_____ DATE FINISHED:_____

GENRE		☆ ☆ ☆ ☆ ☆
CHARACTERS		☆ ☆ ☆ ☆ ☆
PLOT STORY		☆ ☆ ☆ ☆ ☆
READABILITY SCORE		☆ ☆ ☆ ☆ ☆
SUBJECT		☆ ☆ ☆ ☆ ☆

NOTES

FAVORITE QUOTES OF THIS BOOK:

HARDCOVER ☐   PAPERBACK ☐   EBOOK ☐   AUDIOBOOK ☐

OVERALL RATING: ☆ ☆ ☆ ☆ ☆   51

TITLE:_____ PUB DATE:_____

AUTHOR:_____ PAGE COUNT:_____

DATE STARTED:_____ DATE FINISHED:_____

GENRE		☆ ☆ ☆ ☆ ☆
CHARACTERS		☆ ☆ ☆ ☆ ☆
PLOT STORY		☆ ☆ ☆ ☆ ☆
READABILITY SCORE		☆ ☆ ☆ ☆ ☆
SUBJECT		☆ ☆ ☆ ☆ ☆

NOTES

FAVORITE QUOTES OF THIS BOOK:

HARDCOVER ☐   PAPERBACK ☐   EBOOK ☐   AUDIOBOOK ☐

OVERALL RATING: ☆ ☆ ☆ ☆ ☆   52

TITLE:_____ PUB DATE:_____

AUTHOR:_____ PAGE COUNT:_____

DATE STARTED:_____ DATE FINISHED:_____

GENRE		☆ ☆ ☆ ☆ ☆
CHARACTERS		☆ ☆ ☆ ☆ ☆
PLOT STORY		☆ ☆ ☆ ☆ ☆
READABILITY SCORE		☆ ☆ ☆ ☆ ☆
SUBJECT		☆ ☆ ☆ ☆ ☆

NOTES

FAVORITE QUOTES OF THIS BOOK:

HARDCOVER ☐   PAPERBACK ☐   EBOOK ☐   AUDIOBOOK ☐

OVERALL RATING: ☆ ☆ ☆ ☆ ☆   53

TITLE: _____ PUB DATE: _____

AUTHOR: _____ PAGE COUNT: _____

DATE STARTED: _____ DATE FINISHED: _____

GENRE		☆ ☆ ☆ ☆ ☆
CHARACTERS		☆ ☆ ☆ ☆ ☆
PLOT STORY		☆ ☆ ☆ ☆ ☆
READABILITY SCORE		☆ ☆ ☆ ☆ ☆
SUBJECT		☆ ☆ ☆ ☆ ☆

NOTES

FAVORITE QUOTES OF THIS BOOK:

HARDCOVER ☐   PAPERBACK ☐   EBOOK ☐   AUDIOBOOK ☐

OVERALL RATING: ☆ ☆ ☆ ☆ ☆

TITLE:		PUB DATE:
AUTHOR:		PAGE COUNT:
DATE STARTED:	DATE FINISHED:

GENRE		☆ ☆ ☆ ☆ ☆
CHARACTERS		☆ ☆ ☆ ☆ ☆
PLOT STORY		☆ ☆ ☆ ☆ ☆
READABILITY SCORE		☆ ☆ ☆ ☆ ☆
SUBJECT		☆ ☆ ☆ ☆ ☆

NOTES

FAVORITE QUOTES OF THIS BOOK:

HARDCOVER ☐   PAPERBACK ☐   EBOOK ☐   AUDIOBOOK ☐

OVERALL RATING: ☆ ☆ ☆ ☆ ☆

TITLE: _____ PUB DATE: _____

AUTHOR: _____ PAGE COUNT: _____

DATE STARTED: _____ DATE FINISHED: _____

GENRE		☆ ☆ ☆ ☆ ☆
CHARACTERS		☆ ☆ ☆ ☆ ☆
PLOT STORY		☆ ☆ ☆ ☆ ☆
READABILITY SCORE		☆ ☆ ☆ ☆ ☆
SUBJECT		☆ ☆ ☆ ☆ ☆

NOTES

FAVORITE QUOTES OF THIS BOOK:

HARDCOVER ☐   PAPERBACK ☐   EBOOK ☐   AUDIOBOOK ☐

OVERALL RATING: ☆ ☆ ☆ ☆ ☆   56

TITLE:_____ PUB DATE:_____

AUTHOR:_____ PAGE COUNT:_____

DATE STARTED:_____ DATE FINISHED:_____

GENRE		☆ ☆ ☆ ☆ ☆
CHARACTERS		☆ ☆ ☆ ☆ ☆
PLOT STORY		☆ ☆ ☆ ☆ ☆
READABILITY SCORE		☆ ☆ ☆ ☆ ☆
SUBJECT		☆ ☆ ☆ ☆ ☆

NOTES

FAVORITE QUOTES OF THIS BOOK:

HARDCOVER ☐   PAPERBACK ☐   EBOOK ☐   AUDIOBOOK ☐

OVERALL RATING: ☆ ☆ ☆ ☆ ☆

TITLE:_____ PUB DATE:_____

AUTHOR:_____ PAGE COUNT:_____

DATE STARTED:_____ DATE FINISHED:_____

GENRE		☆ ☆ ☆ ☆ ☆
CHARACTERS		☆ ☆ ☆ ☆ ☆
PLOT STORY		☆ ☆ ☆ ☆ ☆
READABILITY SCORE		☆ ☆ ☆ ☆ ☆
SUBJECT		☆ ☆ ☆ ☆ ☆

NOTES

FAVORITE QUOTES OF THIS BOOK:

HARDCOVER ☐   PAPERBACK ☐   EBOOK ☐   AUDIOBOOK ☐

OVERALL RATING: ☆ ☆ ☆ ☆ ☆   58

TITLE:_____ PUB DATE:_____

AUTHOR:_____ PAGE COUNT:_____

DATE STARTED:_____ DATE FINISHED:_____

GENRE		☆ ☆ ☆ ☆ ☆
CHARACTERS		☆ ☆ ☆ ☆ ☆
PLOT STORY		☆ ☆ ☆ ☆ ☆
READABILITY SCORE		☆ ☆ ☆ ☆ ☆
SUBJECT		☆ ☆ ☆ ☆ ☆

NOTES

FAVORITE QUOTES OF THIS BOOK:

HARDCOVER ☐   PAPERBACK ☐   EBOOK ☐   AUDIOBOOK ☐

OVERALL RATING: ☆ ☆ ☆ ☆ ☆   59

TITLE:_____ PUB DATE:_____

AUTHOR:_____ PAGE COUNT:_____

DATE STARTED:_____ DATE FINISHED:_____

GENRE		☆ ☆ ☆ ☆ ☆
CHARACTERS		☆ ☆ ☆ ☆ ☆
PLOT STORY		☆ ☆ ☆ ☆ ☆
READABILITY SCORE		☆ ☆ ☆ ☆ ☆
SUBJECT		☆ ☆ ☆ ☆ ☆

NOTES

FAVORITE QUOTES OF THIS BOOK:

HARDCOVER ☐   PAPERBACK ☐   EBOOK ☐   AUDIOBOOK ☐

OVERALL RATING: ☆ ☆ ☆ ☆ ☆   60

TITLE:_____ PUB DATE:_____

AUTHOR:_____ PAGE COUNT:_____

DATE STARTED:_____ DATE FINISHED:_____

GENRE		☆ ☆ ☆ ☆ ☆
CHARACTERS		☆ ☆ ☆ ☆ ☆
PLOT STORY		☆ ☆ ☆ ☆ ☆
READABILITY SCORE		☆ ☆ ☆ ☆ ☆
SUBJECT		☆ ☆ ☆ ☆ ☆

NOTES

FAVORITE QUOTES OF THIS BOOK:

HARDCOVER ☐   PAPERBACK ☐   EBOOK ☐   AUDIOBOOK ☐

OVERALL RATING: ☆ ☆ ☆ ☆ ☆   61

TITLE: _____ PUB DATE: _____

AUTHOR: _____ PAGE COUNT: _____

DATE STARTED: _____ DATE FINISHED: _____

GENRE		☆ ☆ ☆ ☆ ☆
CHARACTERS		☆ ☆ ☆ ☆ ☆
PLOT STORY		☆ ☆ ☆ ☆ ☆
READABILITY SCORE		☆ ☆ ☆ ☆ ☆
SUBJECT		☆ ☆ ☆ ☆ ☆

NOTES

FAVORITE QUOTES OF THIS BOOK:

HARDCOVER ☐   PAPERBACK ☐   EBOOK ☐   AUDIOBOOK ☐

OVERALL RATING: ☆ ☆ ☆ ☆ ☆   62

TITLE:_____ PUB DATE:_____

AUTHOR:_____ PAGE COUNT:_____

DATE STARTED:_____ DATE FINISHED:_____

GENRE		☆ ☆ ☆ ☆ ☆
CHARACTERS		☆ ☆ ☆ ☆ ☆
PLOT STORY		☆ ☆ ☆ ☆ ☆
READABILITY SCORE		☆ ☆ ☆ ☆ ☆
SUBJECT		☆ ☆ ☆ ☆ ☆

NOTES

FAVORITE QUOTES OF THIS BOOK:

HARDCOVER ☐   PAPERBACK ☐   EBOOK ☐   AUDIOBOOK ☐

OVERALL RATING: ☆ ☆ ☆ ☆ ☆   63

TITLE:			PUB DATE:
AUTHOR:			PAGE COUNT:
DATE STARTED:		DATE FINISHED:	

GENRE		☆ ☆ ☆ ☆ ☆
CHARACTERS		☆ ☆ ☆ ☆ ☆
PLOT STORY		☆ ☆ ☆ ☆ ☆
READABILITY SCORE		☆ ☆ ☆ ☆ ☆
SUBJECT		☆ ☆ ☆ ☆ ☆

NOTES

FAVORITE QUOTES OF THIS BOOK:

HARDCOVER ☐   PAPERBACK ☐   EBOOK ☐   AUDIOBOOK ☐

OVERALL RATING: ☆ ☆ ☆ ☆ ☆   64

TITLE:		PUB DATE:
AUTHOR:		PAGE COUNT:
DATE STARTED:		DATE FINISHED:

GENRE		☆ ☆ ☆ ☆ ☆
CHARACTERS		☆ ☆ ☆ ☆ ☆
PLOT STORY		☆ ☆ ☆ ☆ ☆
READABILITY SCORE		☆ ☆ ☆ ☆ ☆
SUBJECT		☆ ☆ ☆ ☆ ☆

NOTES

FAVORITE QUOTES OF THIS BOOK:

HARDCOVER ☐   PAPERBACK ☐   EBOOK ☐   AUDIOBOOK ☐

OVERALL RATING: ☆ ☆ ☆ ☆ ☆   65

TITLE: _____   PUB DATE: _____

AUTHOR: _____   PAGE COUNT: _____

DATE STARTED: _____   DATE FINISHED: _____

GENRE		☆ ☆ ☆ ☆ ☆
CHARACTERS		☆ ☆ ☆ ☆ ☆
PLOT STORY		☆ ☆ ☆ ☆ ☆
READABILITY SCORE		☆ ☆ ☆ ☆ ☆
SUBJECT		☆ ☆ ☆ ☆ ☆

NOTES

FAVORITE QUOTES OF THIS BOOK:

HARDCOVER ☐   PAPERBACK ☐   EBOOK ☐   AUDIOBOOK ☐

OVERALL RATING: ☆ ☆ ☆ ☆ ☆   66

TITLE:_____ PUB DATE:_____

AUTHOR:_____ PAGE COUNT:_____

DATE STARTED:_____ DATE FINISHED:_____

GENRE		☆ ☆ ☆ ☆ ☆
CHARACTERS		☆ ☆ ☆ ☆ ☆
PLOT STORY		☆ ☆ ☆ ☆ ☆
READABILITY SCORE		☆ ☆ ☆ ☆ ☆
SUBJECT		☆ ☆ ☆ ☆ ☆

NOTES

FAVORITE QUOTES OF THIS BOOK:

HARDCOVER ☐   PAPERBACK ☐   EBOOK ☐   AUDIOBOOK ☐

OVERALL RATING: ☆ ☆ ☆ ☆ ☆   67

TITLE:		PUB DATE:
AUTHOR:		PAGE COUNT:
DATE STARTED:	DATE FINISHED:	

GENRE		☆ ☆ ☆ ☆ ☆
CHARACTERS		☆ ☆ ☆ ☆ ☆
PLOT STORY		☆ ☆ ☆ ☆ ☆
READABILITY SCORE		☆ ☆ ☆ ☆ ☆
SUBJECT		☆ ☆ ☆ ☆ ☆

NOTES

FAVORITE QUOTES OF THIS BOOK:

HARDCOVER ☐ PAPERBACK ☐ EBOOK ☐ AUDIOBOOK ☐

OVERALL RATING: ☆ ☆ ☆ ☆ ☆

TITLE:		PUB DATE:
AUTHOR:		PAGE COUNT:
DATE STARTED:		DATE FINISHED:

GENRE		☆ ☆ ☆ ☆ ☆
CHARACTERS		☆ ☆ ☆ ☆ ☆
PLOT STORY		☆ ☆ ☆ ☆ ☆
READABILITY SCORE		☆ ☆ ☆ ☆ ☆
SUBJECT		☆ ☆ ☆ ☆ ☆

NOTES

FAVORITE QUOTES OF THIS BOOK:

HARDCOVER ☐　　　PAPERBACK ☐　　　EBOOK ☐　　　AUDIOBOOK ☐

OVERALL RATING: ☆ ☆ ☆ ☆ ☆

TITLE:_____ PUB DATE:_____

AUTHOR:_____ PAGE COUNT:_____

DATE STARTED:_____ DATE FINISHED:_____

GENRE		☆ ☆ ☆ ☆ ☆
CHARACTERS		☆ ☆ ☆ ☆ ☆
PLOT STORY		☆ ☆ ☆ ☆ ☆
READABILITY SCORE		☆ ☆ ☆ ☆ ☆
SUBJECT		☆ ☆ ☆ ☆ ☆

NOTES

FAVORITE QUOTES OF THIS BOOK:

HARDCOVER ☐   PAPERBACK ☐   EBOOK ☐   AUDIOBOOK ☐

OVERALL RATING: ☆ ☆ ☆ ☆ ☆   70

TITLE: _____ PUB DATE: _____

AUTHOR: _____ PAGE COUNT: _____

DATE STARTED: _____ DATE FINISHED: _____

GENRE		☆ ☆ ☆ ☆ ☆
CHARACTERS		☆ ☆ ☆ ☆ ☆
PLOT STORY		☆ ☆ ☆ ☆ ☆
READABILITY SCORE		☆ ☆ ☆ ☆ ☆
SUBJECT		☆ ☆ ☆ ☆ ☆

NOTES

FAVORITE QUOTES OF THIS BOOK:

HARDCOVER ☐   PAPERBACK ☐   EBOOK ☐   AUDIOBOOK ☐

OVERALL RATING: ☆ ☆ ☆ ☆ ☆

TITLE:_____ PUB DATE:_____

AUTHOR:_____ PAGE COUNT:_____

DATE STARTED:_____ DATE FINISHED:_____

GENRE		☆ ☆ ☆ ☆ ☆
CHARACTERS		☆ ☆ ☆ ☆ ☆
PLOT STORY		☆ ☆ ☆ ☆ ☆
READABILITY SCORE		☆ ☆ ☆ ☆ ☆
SUBJECT		☆ ☆ ☆ ☆ ☆

NOTES

FAVORITE QUOTES OF THIS BOOK:

HARDCOVER ☐   PAPERBACK ☐   EBOOK ☐   AUDIOBOOK ☐

OVERALL RATING: ☆ ☆ ☆ ☆ ☆

TITLE:		PUB DATE:
AUTHOR:		PAGE COUNT:
DATE STARTED:		DATE FINISHED:

GENRE		☆ ☆ ☆ ☆ ☆
CHARACTERS		☆ ☆ ☆ ☆ ☆
PLOT STORY		☆ ☆ ☆ ☆ ☆
READABILITY SCORE		☆ ☆ ☆ ☆ ☆
SUBJECT		☆ ☆ ☆ ☆ ☆

NOTES

FAVORITE QUOTES OF THIS BOOK:

HARDCOVER ☐   PAPERBACK ☐   EBOOK ☐   AUDIOBOOK ☐

OVERALL RATING: ☆ ☆ ☆ ☆ ☆   73

TITLE:_____ PUB DATE:_____

AUTHOR:_____ PAGE COUNT:_____

DATE STARTED:_____ DATE FINISHED:_____

GENRE		☆ ☆ ☆ ☆ ☆
CHARACTERS		☆ ☆ ☆ ☆ ☆
PLOT STORY		☆ ☆ ☆ ☆ ☆
READABILITY SCORE		☆ ☆ ☆ ☆ ☆
SUBJECT		☆ ☆ ☆ ☆ ☆

NOTES

FAVORITE QUOTES OF THIS BOOK:

HARDCOVER ☐   PAPERBACK ☐   EBOOK ☐   AUDIOBOOK ☐

OVERALL RATING: ☆ ☆ ☆ ☆ ☆   74

TITLE:_____   PUB DATE:_____

AUTHOR:_____   PAGE COUNT:_____

DATE STARTED:_____   DATE FINISHED:_____

GENRE		☆ ☆ ☆ ☆ ☆
CHARACTERS		☆ ☆ ☆ ☆ ☆
PLOT STORY		☆ ☆ ☆ ☆ ☆
READABILITY SCORE		☆ ☆ ☆ ☆ ☆
SUBJECT		☆ ☆ ☆ ☆ ☆

NOTES

FAVORITE QUOTES OF THIS BOOK:

HARDCOVER ☐   PAPERBACK ☐   EBOOK ☐   AUDIOBOOK ☐

OVERALL RATING: ☆ ☆ ☆ ☆ ☆

TITLE: _____ PUB DATE: _____

AUTHOR: _____ PAGE COUNT: _____

DATE STARTED: _____ DATE FINISHED: _____

GENRE		☆ ☆ ☆ ☆ ☆
CHARACTERS		☆ ☆ ☆ ☆ ☆
PLOT STORY		☆ ☆ ☆ ☆ ☆
READABILITY SCORE		☆ ☆ ☆ ☆ ☆
SUBJECT		☆ ☆ ☆ ☆ ☆

NOTES

FAVORITE QUOTES OF THIS BOOK:

HARDCOVER ☐   PAPERBACK ☐   EBOOK ☐   AUDIOBOOK ☐

OVERALL RATING: ☆ ☆ ☆ ☆ ☆

TITLE:_____ PUB DATE:_____

AUTHOR:_____ PAGE COUNT:_____

DATE STARTED:_____ DATE FINISHED:_____

GENRE		☆ ☆ ☆ ☆ ☆
CHARACTERS		☆ ☆ ☆ ☆ ☆
PLOT STORY		☆ ☆ ☆ ☆ ☆
READABILITY SCORE		☆ ☆ ☆ ☆ ☆
SUBJECT		☆ ☆ ☆ ☆ ☆

NOTES

FAVORITE QUOTES OF THIS BOOK:

HARDCOVER ☐   PAPERBACK ☐   EBOOK ☐   AUDIOBOOK ☐

OVERALL RATING: ☆ ☆ ☆ ☆ ☆   77

TITLE:_____ PUB DATE:_____

AUTHOR:_____ PAGE COUNT:_____

DATE STARTED:_____ DATE FINISHED:_____

GENERE		☆ ☆ ☆ ☆ ☆
CHARACTERS		☆ ☆ ☆ ☆ ☆
PLOT STORY		☆ ☆ ☆ ☆ ☆
READABILITY SCORE		☆ ☆ ☆ ☆ ☆
SUBJECT		☆ ☆ ☆ ☆ ☆

NOTES

FAVORITE QUOTES OF THIS BOOK:

HARDCOVER ☐   PAPERBACK ☐   EBOOK ☐   AUDIOBOOK ☐

OVERALL RATING: ☆ ☆ ☆ ☆ ☆   78

TITLE:_____ PUB DATE:_____

AUTHOR:_____ PAGE COUNT:_____

DATE STARTED:_____ DATE FINISHED:_____

GENRE		☆ ☆ ☆ ☆ ☆
CHARACTERS		☆ ☆ ☆ ☆ ☆
PLOT STORY		☆ ☆ ☆ ☆ ☆
READABILITY SCORE		☆ ☆ ☆ ☆ ☆
SUBJECT		☆ ☆ ☆ ☆ ☆

NOTES

FAVORITE QUOTES OF THIS BOOK:

HARDCOVER ☐   PAPERBACK ☐   EBOOK ☐   AUDIOBOOK ☐

OVERALL RATING: ☆ ☆ ☆ ☆ ☆   79

TITLE:_____ PUB DATE:_____

AUTHOR:_____ PAGE COUNT:_____

DATE STARTED:_____ DATE FINISHED:_____

GENRE		☆ ☆ ☆ ☆ ☆
CHARACTERS		☆ ☆ ☆ ☆ ☆
PLOT STORY		☆ ☆ ☆ ☆ ☆
READABILITY SCORE		☆ ☆ ☆ ☆ ☆
SUBJECT		☆ ☆ ☆ ☆ ☆

NOTES

FAVORITE QUOTES OF THIS BOOK:

HARDCOVER ☐   PAPERBACK ☐   EBOOK ☐   AUDIOBOOK ☐

OVERALL RATING: ☆ ☆ ☆ ☆ ☆   80

TITLE: _____	PUB DATE: _____
AUTHOR: _____	PAGE COUNT: _____
DATE STARTED: _____ DATE FINISHED: _____	

GENRE		☆ ☆ ☆ ☆ ☆
CHARACTERS		☆ ☆ ☆ ☆ ☆
PLOT STORY		☆ ☆ ☆ ☆ ☆
READABILITY SCORE		☆ ☆ ☆ ☆ ☆
SUBJECT		☆ ☆ ☆ ☆ ☆

NOTES

FAVORITE QUOTES OF THIS BOOK:

HARDCOVER ☐   PAPERBACK ☐   EBOOK ☐   AUDIOBOOK ☐

OVERALL RATING: ☆ ☆ ☆ ☆ ☆

TITLE:_____ PUB DATE:_____

AUTHOR:_____ PAGE COUNT:_____

DATE STARTED:_____ DATE FINISHED:_____

GENRE		☆ ☆ ☆ ☆ ☆
CHARACTERS		☆ ☆ ☆ ☆ ☆
PLOT STORY		☆ ☆ ☆ ☆ ☆
READABILITY SCORE		☆ ☆ ☆ ☆ ☆
SUBJECT		☆ ☆ ☆ ☆ ☆

NOTES

FAVORITE QUOTES OF THIS BOOK:

HARDCOVER ☐   PAPERBACK ☐   EBOOK ☐   AUDIOBOOK ☐

OVERALL RATING: ☆ ☆ ☆ ☆ ☆   82

TITLE:_____ PUB DATE:_____

AUTHOR:_____ PAGE COUNT:_____

DATE STARTED:_____ DATE FINISHED:_____

GENRE		☆ ☆ ☆ ☆ ☆
CHARACTERS		☆ ☆ ☆ ☆ ☆
PLOT STORY		☆ ☆ ☆ ☆ ☆
READABILITY SCORE		☆ ☆ ☆ ☆ ☆
SUBJECT		☆ ☆ ☆ ☆ ☆

NOTES

FAVORITE QUOTES OF THIS BOOK:

HARDCOVER ☐ PAPERBACK ☐ EBOOK ☐ AUDIOBOOK ☐

OVERALL RATING: ☆ ☆ ☆ ☆ ☆

TITLE:_____ PUB DATE:_____

AUTHOR:_____ PAGE COUNT:_____

DATE STARTED:_____ DATE FINISHED:_____

GENERE		☆ ☆ ☆ ☆ ☆
CHARACTERS		☆ ☆ ☆ ☆ ☆
PLOT STORY		☆ ☆ ☆ ☆ ☆
READABILITY SCORE		☆ ☆ ☆ ☆ ☆
SUBJECT		☆ ☆ ☆ ☆ ☆

NOTES

FAVORITE QUOTES OF THIS BOOK:

HARDCOVER ☐   PAPERBACK ☐   EBOOK ☐   AUDIOBOOK ☐

OVERALL RATING: ☆ ☆ ☆ ☆ ☆

TITLE:_____ PUB DATE:_____

AUTHOR:_____ PAGE COUNT:_____

DATE STARTED:_____ DATE FINISHED:_____

GENRE		☆ ☆ ☆ ☆ ☆
CHARACTERS		☆ ☆ ☆ ☆ ☆
PLOT STORY		☆ ☆ ☆ ☆ ☆
READABILITY SCORE		☆ ☆ ☆ ☆ ☆
SUBJECT		☆ ☆ ☆ ☆ ☆

NOTES

FAVORITE QUOTES OF THIS BOOK:

HARDCOVER ☐　　　PAPERBACK ☐　　　EBOOK ☐　　　AUDIOBOOK ☐

OVERALL RATING: ☆ ☆ ☆ ☆ ☆

TITLE: _____	PUB DATE: _____
AUTHOR: _____	PAGE COUNT: _____
DATE STARTED: _____ DATE FINISHED: _____	

GENRE		☆ ☆ ☆ ☆ ☆
CHARACTERS		☆ ☆ ☆ ☆ ☆
PLOT STORY		☆ ☆ ☆ ☆ ☆
READABILITY SCORE		☆ ☆ ☆ ☆ ☆
SUBJECT		☆ ☆ ☆ ☆ ☆

NOTES

FAVORITE QUOTES OF THIS BOOK:

HARDCOVER ☐   PAPERBACK ☐   EBOOK ☐   AUDIOBOOK ☐

OVERALL RATING: ☆ ☆ ☆ ☆ ☆

TITLE:_____ PUB DATE:_____

AUTHOR:_____ PAGE COUNT:_____

DATE STARTED:_____ DATE FINISHED:_____

GENRE		☆ ☆ ☆ ☆ ☆
CHARACTERS		☆ ☆ ☆ ☆ ☆
PLOT STORY		☆ ☆ ☆ ☆ ☆
READABILITY SCORE		☆ ☆ ☆ ☆ ☆
SUBJECT		☆ ☆ ☆ ☆ ☆

NOTES

FAVORITE QUOTES OF THIS BOOK:

HARDCOVER ☐   PAPERBACK ☐   EBOOK ☐   AUDIOBOOK ☐

OVERALL RATING: ☆ ☆ ☆ ☆ ☆

TITLE:_____ PUB DATE:_____

AUTHOR:_____ PAGE COUNT:_____

DATE STARTED:_____ DATE FINISHED:_____

GENRE		☆ ☆ ☆ ☆ ☆
CHARACTERS		☆ ☆ ☆ ☆ ☆
PLOT STORY		☆ ☆ ☆ ☆ ☆
READABILITY SCORE		☆ ☆ ☆ ☆ ☆
SUBJECT		☆ ☆ ☆ ☆ ☆

NOTES

FAVORITE QUOTES OF THIS BOOK:

HARDCOVER ☐   PAPERBACK ☐   EBOOK ☐   AUDIOBOOK ☐

OVERALL RATING: ☆ ☆ ☆ ☆ ☆

TITLE:		PUB DATE:
AUTHOR:		PAGE COUNT:
DATE STARTED:		DATE FINISHED:

GENRE		☆ ☆ ☆ ☆ ☆
CHARACTERS		☆ ☆ ☆ ☆ ☆
PLOT STORY		☆ ☆ ☆ ☆ ☆
READABILITY SCORE		☆ ☆ ☆ ☆ ☆
SUBJECT		☆ ☆ ☆ ☆ ☆

NOTES

FAVORITE QUOTES OF THIS BOOK:

HARDCOVER ☐   PAPERBACK ☐   EBOOK ☐   AUDIOBOOK ☐

OVERALL RATING: ☆ ☆ ☆ ☆ ☆

TITLE:_____ PUB DATE:_____

AUTHOR:_____ PAGE COUNT:_____

DATE STARTED:_____ DATE FINISHED:_____

GENRE		☆ ☆ ☆ ☆ ☆
CHARACTERS		☆ ☆ ☆ ☆ ☆
PLOT STORY		☆ ☆ ☆ ☆ ☆
READABILITY SCORE		☆ ☆ ☆ ☆ ☆
SUBJECT		☆ ☆ ☆ ☆ ☆

NOTES

FAVORITE QUOTES OF THIS BOOK:

HARDCOVER ☐   PAPERBACK ☐   EBOOK ☐   AUDIOBOOK ☐

OVERALL RATING: ☆ ☆ ☆ ☆ ☆   90

TITLE: _____ PUB DATE: _____

AUTHOR: _____ PAGE COUNT: _____

DATE STARTED: _____ DATE FINISHED: _____

GENRE		☆ ☆ ☆ ☆ ☆
CHARACTERS		☆ ☆ ☆ ☆ ☆
PLOT STORY		☆ ☆ ☆ ☆ ☆
READABILITY SCORE		☆ ☆ ☆ ☆ ☆
SUBJECT		☆ ☆ ☆ ☆ ☆

NOTES

FAVORITE QUOTES OF THIS BOOK:

HARDCOVER ☐   PAPERBACK ☐   EBOOK ☐   AUDIOBOOK ☐

OVERALL RATING: ☆ ☆ ☆ ☆ ☆

TITLE:		PUB DATE:
AUTHOR:		PAGE COUNT:
DATE STARTED:	DATE FINISHED:	

GENRE		☆ ☆ ☆ ☆ ☆
CHARACTERS		☆ ☆ ☆ ☆ ☆
PLOT STORY		☆ ☆ ☆ ☆ ☆
READABILITY SCORE		☆ ☆ ☆ ☆ ☆
SUBJECT		☆ ☆ ☆ ☆ ☆

NOTES

FAVORITE QUOTES OF THIS BOOK:

HARDCOVER ☐   PAPERBACK ☐   EBOOK ☐   AUDIOBOOK ☐

OVERALL RATING: ☆ ☆ ☆ ☆ ☆   92

TITLE:_____ PUB DATE:_____

AUTHOR:_____ PAGE COUNT:_____

DATE STARTED:_____ DATE FINISHED:_____

GENRE		☆ ☆ ☆ ☆ ☆
CHARACTERS		☆ ☆ ☆ ☆ ☆
PLOT STORY		☆ ☆ ☆ ☆ ☆
READABILITY SCORE		☆ ☆ ☆ ☆ ☆
SUBJECT		☆ ☆ ☆ ☆ ☆

NOTES

FAVORITE QUOTES OF THIS BOOK:

HARDCOVER ☐   PAPERBACK ☐   EBOOK ☐   AUDIOBOOK ☐

OVERALL RATING: ☆ ☆ ☆ ☆ ☆   93

TITLE:_____ PUB DATE:_____

AUTHOR:_____ PAGE COUNT:_____

DATE STARTED:_____ DATE FINISHED:_____

GENRE		☆ ☆ ☆ ☆ ☆
CHARACTERS		☆ ☆ ☆ ☆ ☆
PLOT STORY		☆ ☆ ☆ ☆ ☆
READABILITY SCORE		☆ ☆ ☆ ☆ ☆
SUBJECT		☆ ☆ ☆ ☆ ☆

NOTES

FAVORITE QUOTES OF THIS BOOK:

HARDCOVER ☐   PAPERBACK ☐   EBOOK ☐   AUDIOBOOK ☐

OVERALL RATING: ☆ ☆ ☆ ☆ ☆   94

TITLE: _____ PUB DATE: _____

AUTHOR: _____ PAGE COUNT: _____

DATE STARTED: _____ DATE FINISHED: _____

GENERE		☆ ☆ ☆ ☆ ☆
CHARACTERS		☆ ☆ ☆ ☆ ☆
PLOT STORY		☆ ☆ ☆ ☆ ☆
READABILITY SCORE		☆ ☆ ☆ ☆ ☆
SUBJECT		☆ ☆ ☆ ☆ ☆

NOTES

FAVORITE QUOTES OF THIS BOOK:

HARDCOVER ☐   PAPERBACK ☐   EBOOK ☐   AUDIOBOOK ☐

OVERALL RATING: ☆ ☆ ☆ ☆ ☆

TITLE:_____ PUB DATE:_____

AUTHOR:_____ PAGE COUNT:_____

DATE STARTED:_____ DATE FINISHED:_____

GENRE		☆ ☆ ☆ ☆ ☆
CHARACTERS		☆ ☆ ☆ ☆ ☆
PLOT STORY		☆ ☆ ☆ ☆ ☆
READABILITY SCORE		☆ ☆ ☆ ☆ ☆
SUBJECT		☆ ☆ ☆ ☆ ☆

NOTES

FAVORITE QUOTES OF THIS BOOK:

HARDCOVER ☐   PAPERBACK ☐   EBOOK ☐   AUDIOBOOK ☐

OVERALL RATING: ☆ ☆ ☆ ☆ ☆

TITLE:_____ PUB DATE:_____

AUTHOR:_____ PAGE COUNT:_____

DATE STARTED:_____ DATE FINISHED:_____

GENRE		☆ ☆ ☆ ☆ ☆
CHARACTERS		☆ ☆ ☆ ☆ ☆
PLOT STORY		☆ ☆ ☆ ☆ ☆
READABILITY SCORE		☆ ☆ ☆ ☆ ☆
SUBJECT		☆ ☆ ☆ ☆ ☆

NOTES

FAVORITE QUOTES OF THIS BOOK:

HARDCOVER ☐   PAPERBACK ☐   EBOOK ☐   AUDIOBOOK ☐

OVERALL RATING: ☆ ☆ ☆ ☆ ☆   97

TITLE: _____ PUB DATE: _____

AUTHOR: _____ PAGE COUNT: _____

DATE STARTED: _____ DATE FINISHED: _____

GENERE		☆ ☆ ☆ ☆ ☆
CHARACTERS		☆ ☆ ☆ ☆ ☆
PLOT STORY		☆ ☆ ☆ ☆ ☆
READABILITY SCORE		☆ ☆ ☆ ☆ ☆
SUBJECT		☆ ☆ ☆ ☆ ☆

NOTES

FAVORITE QUOTES OF THIS BOOK:

HARDCOVER ☐   PAPERBACK ☐   EBOOK ☐   AUDIOBOOK ☐

OVERALL RATING: ☆ ☆ ☆ ☆ ☆

TITLE:_____ PUB DATE:_____

AUTHOR:_____ PAGE COUNT:_____

DATE STARTED:_____ DATE FINISHED:_____

GENERE		☆ ☆ ☆ ☆ ☆
CHARACTERS		☆ ☆ ☆ ☆ ☆
PLOT STORY		☆ ☆ ☆ ☆ ☆
READABILITY SCORE		☆ ☆ ☆ ☆ ☆
SUBJECT		☆ ☆ ☆ ☆ ☆

NOTES

FAVORITE QUOTES OF THIS BOOK:

HARDCOVER ☐   PAPERBACK ☐   EBOOK ☐   AUDIOBOOK ☐

OVERALL RATING: ☆ ☆ ☆ ☆ ☆   99

TITLE:_____ PUB DATE:_____

AUTHOR:_____ PAGE COUNT:_____

DATE STARTED:_____ DATE FINISHED:_____

GENRE		☆ ☆ ☆ ☆ ☆
CHARACTERS		☆ ☆ ☆ ☆ ☆
PLOT STORY		☆ ☆ ☆ ☆ ☆
READABILITY SCORE		☆ ☆ ☆ ☆ ☆
SUBJECT		☆ ☆ ☆ ☆ ☆

NOTES

FAVORITE QUOTES OF THIS BOOK:

HARDCOVER ☐   PAPERBACK ☐   EBOOK ☐   AUDIOBOOK ☐

OVERALL RATING: ☆ ☆ ☆ ☆ ☆

Made in the USA
Monee, IL
05 December 2020